A Musician's Dictionary

A Musician's Dictionary

David W. Barber
Dave Donald

Author's Note and Acknowledgements

As work progressed on this book and before I had decided upon its title, I grew tired of having constantly to refer to it as "my book" or "the book I'm working on." And so it came to be known simply as SAM—which doesn't stand for anything; it was just that I already had a book named FRED in the works, and SAM was more polite than "hey you." And so it is as SAM that I still know it. It still usually answers to that name.

There are many people who — by way of advice, encouragement or otherwise-were helpful at various stages in the production of this book. To them I offer my warmest acknowledgements and thanks. Chief among these are the members of my family and my friends for their support and encouragement.

The above two paragraphs were written in 1985, this one in 1990. The prospect of a revised publishing format has allowed me the chance to make a few revisions. Nothing major, but I've added some new definitions and expanded a few others. It also gave us a chance to tinker around with punctuation and other aspects of the book's presentation — thereby (I hope) banishing all the previous gremlins, though doubtless introducing some new ones in the process. Thanks are due to Sound And Vision publisher Geoff Savage for his continuing efforts. Thankfully, he likes to tinker too.

DWB
Kingston, 1985/1990

About the Authors

David Barber would like to admit that he is a close relative of the famous American composer Samuel Barber, but honesty prevents him from doing so. Barber lives in Kingston, Ontario where he is the entertainment editor for The Whig-Standard. In his spare time, he is a freelance composer and performer.

Dave Donald can't remember when he didn't scrawl his little markes on most surfaces, so it doesn't come as much of a surprise that he now makes a living doing just that. He is currently balancing a steady job as art director for a Toronto magazine publisher with his other more abstruse artistic pursuits.

Preface

Those wedded to music belong to the realm of the constant-ephemeral — a visionary realm requiring oft-time the painful renunciation of reality — remember those glorious images of spirit rendered flesh — of divinity — of beauty of princes and princesses condemned to a yearning for even the shortest-lived mortal incarnation — and oft-times lending that alternative dimension, introspective or objective, as the case may be, to one's own life.

A musician's humour is the inevitable distillation of a capacity to listen to himself, honestly to take blame for his own mistakes and shortcomings, a freedom from prejudice and an ability to see himself in as unreal and ludicrous a light as others might see him, this extra-terrestrial being — messenger, clown, seer, priest or demon - exposing and liberating us to ourselves in the deepest sense possible and without the accusatory embarrassment of words.

For humour is the gift of the Gods — born of deep humanity, of suffering and compassion, as of that divine and somewhat remote disattachment it promotes the same creative originality of observation which reveals the mysteries of nature to the born scientist as the mysteries of human nature to the born artist.

Musicians are, generally, irrepressible in their exuberance, passion and curiosity. Usually, if they are real musicians, they are, as such, essential and irresistible to their mortal fellow-women and fellow-men. They form a curious breed blessed with the eye and ear of the beholder, thus able to make fun of themselves and perhaps, more through humour than philosophy, cheat, if only fleetingly, the very powers of darkness and tragedy which stalk the path of life.

This amusing and witty book has only one ommission, i.e the pianist, who, as a genuinely profound musician taking my teasing in good grace, must be a magician. Having a brilliant pianist as my son, Jeremy by name, my imagination has been exhaustively exercised in commenting — of course disparagingly (for that is the very essence of humour) — on this out-of-tune piece of furniture, which can serve in so many other capacities than music, for instance a bar or nice flat surface to stretch out on, as the case may be; shark-like it displays a menacing lower denture of black and white teeth; a more rational disposition of this lower denture in the proper half-circle has been tried but abandoned, no doubt owing to the increased difficulty of turning pages — also called keyboard, to which the pianist, countering with an upper denture of ill-fitting and bleeding fingers, hammers and grinds out (with the help of additional hammers hidden in the bowel of the beast) a percussive noise of simultaneous notes, called harmony — obviously so dubbed because these notes are in fact short-lived, falsely pitched, and aggressive. Therefore the great pianist is, as I tell my son Jeremy, a good magician, for by sheer will and imagination he conveys the ecstasy of music through means which are therefore a compromise. The keyboard has never developed into a proper typewriter, for the alphabet is unmarked and in no case extends beyond the letter G, and it is further devoid of numerals. For these reasons pianists do not make successful secretaries. I am in no dout that the publisher is reserving an entire book on this vast subject.

And now, having attempted to throw a spadeful of grit into this delightful book, may I offer my best wishes to the reader, who will share and perchance enjoy a sample of musician's humour — from one of this laugh-able stock.

Yehudi Menuhin

Dedication

For Brian Law, who first taught me
that music can laugh, with all due respect.

Le monde est plein de fous,
et qui n'en veut pas voir,
doit se tenir tout seul,
et casser son miroir.

Thomas Love Peacock
(*Crotchet Castle*, 1831)

Audience Participation

Accidentals: Wrong notes.

Acoustics: The science of sound, and the study of how music misbehaves in various physical environments. Most useful as a scapegoat to explain why the performer(s) sound bad — "How can anyone perform in a space like this?" and so on.

Air: 1. A simple tune, often for singer.

2. What the singer must inhale before performing such a tune.

3. In the plural (airs), what the singer puts on after performing such a tune particularly well.

Aleatoric Music: Any form of music composition (but especially in modern music) that relies upon elements of chance for its production — such as provided by the tossing of coins, throwing of dice, or disbursement of artistic grants.

Analysis: 1. A fruitless attempt at musical dissection, similar to autopsy — the result in both cases being a lifeless, dismembered corpse. The practice of music analysis is largely based upon George Bernard Shaw's precept that "He who can, does. He who cannot, teaches."

2. What is required by many musicians, especially those who have studied music analysis.

Applause: Noise made by the audience (often at the wrong time, such as in the middle of a symphony, between movements). Intended to signify congratulations, it is used almost as often to destroy the mood of a quiet piece of music, and to express a desire to end the performance and go home.

Aria: The product of multiplying the singer's length by his or her width.

Artistic Grants: Huge sums of money given at the drop of a hat for useless musical endeavours. They are always given to *other* musicians.

Arts Council: The living embodiment of Murphy's Law ("If something can go wrong, it will") and the paramount example of Man's inhumanity to Man.

Atonality: A pathological disease that affects many composers of modern music. Its most noticeable symptom is the inability to make decisions. It is the advanced and sometimes fatal stage of polytonality.

Audience: A group consisting of individuals who, when afflicted by a cold, do not go to a doctor. They go instead to the concert hall, where they hack and wheeze to their heart's content. Audiences can be divided into two categories: those who sleep with their mouths open, and those who sleep with their mouths closed.

B

Bar: 1. The basic measurement of music, dividing it into sections of an approximately equal number of beats, based upon the reasonable assumption that musicians cannot count higher than four.

2. A place of camaraderie and alcoholic consumption often frequented by musicians (and singers) before, during, and after a performance.

Baritone: The male voice that lies between the Bass and the Tenor (not unlike a shortstop in baseball), combining the negative qualities of both. Baritones have a tendency to sing a different piece of music from everyone else, and to sound like a trombone filled with cold coffee. The term is possibly derived from the Latin *boro*, which means 'dunce.' Most of those who think they are Tenors are actually Baritones, just as most Baritones are really Basses.

Baroque: 1. A period of music so called because the study of it leads to impoverishment.

2. A slang term of encouragement used by musicians. Best exemplified by the phrase "Go for Baroque."

Bass: The lowest vocal line, sung by men, usually old and doddering, often also blind and deaf. Basses have a tendency to sing flat, or not at all, and to sound like a pregnant foghorn. Derived from the Latin *bassus*, which means 'base' (but whether in the sense of 'pedestal' or 'debauched' is not entirely clear).

Bassoon: A low-pitched wind instrument, a relative of the baboon, the buffoon, and the bazooka. Also easily converted into a periscope. The Italian term for bassoon is *fagotto* — which doesn't mean what you think it does.

Baton: The thin white stick used by conductors to establish the beat. Thought to have been derived from some sort of ancient fertility symbol, it is now used chiefly out of longstanding tradition. In fact, it is almost utterly useless, since nobody can actually see it. It is useful, however, for threatening recalcitrant musicians or singers, and ought to be sharpened regularly. Derived from the Latin *bastum*, from which we also get the word 'bastard.'

Beat: 1. The basic unit of measurement in music. It varies from piece to piece, from performance to performance, and from person to person. Using a complicated algebraic formula — based upon sum totals, averages, and phases of the moon — the beat is established by the conductor, and then promptly ignored by all.
2. What a performer is after a performance.

A Baroque Composer

A Bass

Brain: A large human organ that controls thought and reason. Distinguishes Man from lower animals and musicians from the rest of Mankind. In accordance with the principles of Darwin's theory of natural selection and evolution, the cranial space normally reserved for the brain is, in musicians, given over to lung capacity (so that they have, quite literally, blown their brains out). In singers, the absence of brain matter leaves extra room for resonance. Science has been unable to discover whether conductors have been provided with any sort of replacement for the missing brain, but that is highly unlikely.

Brass: 1. A family of orchestral instruments that includes trumpets, trombones, French Horns, and antique bedsteads. The development of brass instruments can be traced back to early twelfth-century cisterns. Sound is produced by means of blowing or buzzing (the so-called 'raspberry' or 'Bronx cheer') into one end of a long, curved tube, in the hopes that the sound that comes out the other end will be less rude. In between may be any number of valves, crooks, spigots, *etc.* In essence, brass instruments are nothing more than elaborate spitoons.

2. Richard Strauss had this piece of advice for would-be conductors: "Never, under any circumstances, *never* look at the brass."

C

Cadence: A device for stopping a piece of music, the musical equivalent of a brick wall. Some cadences are less complete than others, and may be called 'deceptive' or 'unfair' cadences. The most common form of cadence is the one called 'V - I'. In order to understand this, it is necessary to understand the terms 'V' and 'I'.

Cello: A member of the String family, larger than both the violin and the viola. The cello is the instrument said to resemble the human voice most closely. However, it has been unable so far to grasp even the most basic principles of grammar and syntax. This is unfortunate, since its incapacity for witty conversation precludes what might otherwise have been an enjoyable lifestyle spent at dinner parties and on the talk-show circuit.

Choir: A musical organization thought to have been invented by G.F. Handel to assure the perpetuation of performances of *Messiah*.

Church: 1. That institution largely responsible for the existence of choirs, choirmasters, organs, and organists. It is also to blame for sermons, offertories, and other forms of punishment.
           2. The large, damp, draft edifice that houses any or all of the above.

Coloratura Soprano: A Soprano with hiccups.

Compass: 1. Another term for range; *i.e* . all the notes, from lowest to highest, that an instrument is capable of playing, or a singer singing. Does not include screeches or squawks.

2. A device used by campers, to avoid becoming lost. Unfortunately, not applicable to musicians, except while on tour.

Composer: The individual, preferably now dead (the longer the better, up to a point), who was responsible for writing the music. All of the composer's wishes regarding notes, tempo, expression and so on are carefully taken down in the score, and then ignored.

Concert Hall: A place where many individuals go only at times when they want to remove the paper wrappings from candy bars.

Concert Pitch: In the early history of music, pitch was not standardized. It varied from country to country, and even from city to city. This made life very difficult for musicians who wanted to travel. Finally, after many attempts, a committee agreed in 1939 that pitch would be universally standardized. It was based upon A at 440 cycles per second. This made things much simpler for eveyone, since they now all knew exactly what it was they were ignoring. Nowadays, A may be anywhere from 425 to 450. Everyone agrees that concert pitch is a marvelous idea.

Concerto: A sort of musical boxing match between one musician (the soloist) and all the rest (the orchestra), with the conductor acting as referee, in which nobody wins — especially the audience.

Conductor: The person at the front of the orchestra or choir, facing away from the audience (usually out of embarrassment). The musical conductor should not be confused with the railway conductor, who probably has more training. In music, the conductor's primary function is to imitate a windmill, for the aesthetic effect. The conductor's chief weapon is the baton, which everyone is pretending to watch carefully. If the performance goes well, the conductor takes all the credit; if badly, the performers get the blame.

Consonants: A subject of manic obsession among choirmasters. It is said that, by their use, one word may be distinguished from another. The origin of this myth is lost in the mists of Time, and has never been successfully proven, since it is far beyond the capabilities of any singer.

Consumption: 1. A disease that is supposed to effect operatic Sopranos in the role of Mimi (in Puccini's *La Bohème*). The audience is forced to accept that a 200-pound woman who sings for four hours is wasting away.

2. The act of reverence which unites musicians and alcohol in large quantities.

A Conductor

Contralto: The second-highest vocal line sung by women. Contraltos have a tendency to sing flat, and to sound like old molasses pudding. Derived from the Latin *altus*, which means 'high,' but which originally meant 'overfed.'

Copyist: A person hired by composers to transcribe pages of their illegible notation into other pages of the copyist's own notation, equally illegible.

Counterpoint: A musical device similar to needlepoint, although not designed to be hung upon the wall or used on seatcovers. Said to be a musical conversation, it more often resembles an argument. A favorite device of many Baroque composers, all of whom are now dead, although a direct connection between these two facts has never been conclusively established. Although no longer in practice by modern composers, it is still taught in schools, as a form of punishment.

Counter-tenor: The highest adult male voice currently available through legal and moral means. Sings roughly the same range as the Contralto, although he can sing lower if pressed, and higher if pinched. Counter-tenors have a tendency to sing on pitch, but out of rhythm, and to sound like a cross between an oboe and a buzz-saw. Derived from the Latin *contra tenore*, which means 'against Tenors.'

Counterpoint

Critic: Most critics are themselves frustrated musicians who now bear a continual grudge against their more successful (?) colleagues. They are usually employed by newspapers, and their job consists of attending a performance and then producing a written pronouncement upon its quality. Because these articles are continually written under the pressure of deadlines, at a time late at night after the performance when the critic would much rather be asleep comfortably in bed, reviews more often than not reflect an attitude of crankiness and bad temper. On the rare occasions that the critic writes a favourable review, the performers are so overjoyed that they forgive all the nasty things said in the past — at least until the next time the critic pans their performance.

Crook: 1. A curved tube, part of a brass instrument, used for storing spit prior to its disposal onto the floor.
2. The type of person ideally suited for arts management.

Cross relation: An angry relative.

D

Da Capo Aria: A particular type of aria with a built-in repeat, most often found in oratorio, opera, and excess. Much favoured by vain singers — there is no other kind — who are thus assured of at least one encore. Choirs have been known to stand up in the middle, to the confusion of the audience, who then applaud half-heartedly.

Diction: That part of a singer's performance which may be complimented when everything else is horrible. What most people really mean when they say diction is enunciation. Diction means the words chosen; enunciation means the clarity of their utterance. There is no sense complimenting singers on their diction, since the singers had nothing to do with the writing of the text. Trying to maintain this distinction, however, is a fruitless activity.

Discord: 1. Not to be confused with datchord.
2. The emotional state that usually exists amongst a group of musicians, especially with regard to those in authority.

Dominant: What parents must be if they expect their small children to practise for music lessons.

Double-bass:　　(Editor's note: The information contained in this entry is unavailable, due to an injunction against the author successfully obtained by the *Society for the Prevention of Cruelty to Double-Basses and the People Who Play Them*. The legal battles continue, but it is the Editor's hope that subsequent editions of this dictionary will be able to include this information in full.)

Drums:　　A percussion instrument originally played on the battlefield to inspire the troops and frighten the enemy. Even in modern times drums retain their military connotations, being chiefly played by teenagers who wish to frighten their parents or by those wanting to do battle with the neighbours.

E

Encore: A nasty method by which performers get back at the audience for its feigned appreciation in the form of applause. It consists of performing an extra piece "off the cuff" (which has been slavishly prepared for weeks). Audiences would be well advised not to applaud at all, so that everyone can get home that much sooner.

English Horn: A woodwind instrument so named because it is neither English, nor a horn. Not to be confused with the French Horn, which is German.

Ensemble: 1. (*n.*) Any group of individual performers who are supposed to function as a unit.

2. (*adj.*) The feeling of co-operation and togetherness that such groups lack.

Enunciation: What is usually meant by the use of the term Diction (*q.v.*).

Exposition: In a fugue, the exposition is the musical equivalent of having wallpaper that matches the furniture.

The English Horn

F

False Relation: The kind of relative who is supportive of one's musical career only if one is making money.

Fifth: A convenient quantity of alcohol to be consumed before, during or after a performance. (See Bar, 2.)

Fitzwilliam Virginal Book: The famous book belonging to a notorious sixteenth-century rake, cad, and womanizer named Thomas William Orlando Fitzwilliam, who was said to enjoy a challenge. It contains a list of the most desirable and innocent young ladies of Elizabethan London. Fitzwilliam died of old age and exhaustion, the day after his twenty-third birthday.

Flat :   An adjective used to describe a tone that is slightly below pitch. This term ought to be used cautiously, so as not to offend anyone, especially when applied to a woman.

Flats: Little marks that look like this: ♭ and which resemble small b's that have been deflated, or sat upon. They are similar to sharps, but different. Their function is to lower a note by a semi-tone (more or less). When gathered together at the beginning of a line, they form a key signature. This means that each corresponding note should be lowered by a semi-tone

The Making of Flats

whenever it occurs, or whenever the performer remembers to do so. The double-flat lowers the note by two semi-tones, or one whole tone. This latter confusing distinction was invented solely to provide work for theorists and publishers.

Flute: A sophisticated pea-shooter with a range up to five hundred yards and deadly accuracy in close quarters. Blown transversely to confuse the enemy, it can be dismantled into three small pieces, for easy concealment.

Form: 1. The shape of a compostion.
2. The shape of the musician who plays the composition.
3. The piece of paper that must be completed in triplicate (known as ternary form) in order for the musician to get enough money from the arts council to play the compostion.

French Horn: A brass instrument that resembles a snail, but sometimes moves more quickly. The complicated instrument of today is a direct descendant of the early horn used by hunters. It was originally long and straight, but got its present shape when trod upon by a horse. The French Horn is actually German, and should not be confused with the English Horn, which is French.

Fugue: A type of Baroque composition similar to a crossword puzzle, but with fewer clues. The greatest fugue composer was J.S. Bach, who died before completing his seminal work, *The Art of Fugue*. Many musicians since have died trying to play it. (One misguided musicologist who thought that Fugue was actually an 18th-century portrait painter was unceremoniously drummed out of the profession, and has since made a fortune writing record-liner notes.)

G

Glissando: The musical equivalent of stepping on a banana peel.

Grace-note: Every once in a while, the solo performer will attempt an interval, jumping from one note to another. In many instances, this is mere guesswork. If the wrong note is landed upon, the performer may attempt to slide up or down to the correct one. The resulting confusion is politely called a grace-note.

Gregorian Chant: A type of unison singing invented by monks as a mask for snoring.

Groves, Sir George: Only one of many persons who may be turning over in their graves at this point.

Glissando

H

Harmony: A sort of musical sociology: the study of the inter-relationship of individual notes, and how they react in group encounters, such as tone-clusters and orgies. Theorists and others who study harmony have developed a highly intricate system of confusing terminology, to disguise the fact that they really don't know what's going on. The aspiring student of harmony should practise saying phrases such as "secondary sub-mediant appoggiatura six-four" or "first-inversion Neapolitan five-seven of five, sharp four plus eleven going to a half-diminished seven of six" until they sound convincing. If unable to do this in a convincing manner, you may be in the wrong profession, or ought at least to consider becoming a critic, where even the most rudimentary knowledge of music is not needed. It may, in fact, be a hindrance.

Harpsichord: A type of keyboard instrument, a precurser of the piano, and cursed at ever since. Its sound has been described by Sir Thomas Beecham as that of "two skeletons copulating on a corrugated tin roof."

Hemiola: A rhythmic device similar to a hernia.

I

Instrument: That object by which many musicians make noise and earn their livelihoods. To a certain extent, a player can improve merely by replacing an old instrument with a better one.   Similarly, orchestras can be made better by replacing some players with better ones. This never happens as often as it should. Instruments, like their players, come in various shapes and sizes, and various degrees of unpleasantness.

Interval: 1. The distance, real or imagined, between two notes.

2. The British term for intermission: the break that gives the performers a chance to go to the bathroom, and the audience a chance to sneak out early.

3. The waiting period between a performer's previous entry and the next. May vary from one bar to forever.

An Interval

K

Kettledrums: Despite their name, these drums are not very useful for making coffee or tea, since they are far too large, and would take too long to boil the water. This is regrettable, since they are not much use for anything else. Several composers in the past have used kettledrums to imitate sounds of battle and of rumbling thunder. Nowadays, they are used increasingly to imitate certain of the grosser bodily functions. Other than that, percussionists find them useful tables for chessboards.

Key: Certain musical terms defy easy definition. This is one of them.

Key Signature: As explained above (see Flats), a key signature is the attempt to organize what would otherwise be an unruly mob of accidentals into some sort of order at the beginning of each line of the staff. These sharps or flats (but rarely both) may number from none to seven, and their order and placement on the staff are rigidly controlled by music publishers, who are now too lazy to change their established typesetting. Several mnemonic phrases exist to help the musician remember the proper order of accidentals, the most useful being "Father Christmas gets diarrhoea after eating biscuits" for the flats (or is it the sharps?) and — actually, we can't recall the other one.

Klavierstück: A term used by German furniture movers attempting to get a piano through a narrow doorway.

The Kettledrum

L

Laryngitis: The second-most effective and convincing way to silence a singer. The most effective way is death — though somewhat drastic, perhaps. It is only one of a large number of similar afflictions — such as the flu, colds, strep throat, and *delirium tremens* — all of which have been known to affect singers at the least-opportune times. Such catastrophes are extremely prevalent amongst solists, and have been known to lay waste to entire choirs at Christmas time.

Lay-clerk: This term, used to describe certain types of singers in English cathedral and college choirs, is actually not nearly as rude as it may appear.

Lute: A stringed instrument of the Medieval and Renaissance periods, resembling a bloated guitar. It was frequently used to provide background music at mealtimes. It can have as many as sixteen sets of strings (most of them in pairs), which are referred to as 'courses.' (With sixteen courses at mealtime, no wonder it was bloated.) It gets its name from the Arabic *el oude*, the meaning of which has, until recently, eluded musicologists — who are the only ones who would care, anyway. It is now known that the name comes from the practice of using this instrument to accompany lewd songs.

M

Madrigal: A type of part-song, popular in the Renaissance, for unaccompanied voices. Often involves one of the earliest examples of censorship in music: some of the refrains were so lewd and suggestive that they had to be replaced by repetitions of "fa-la-la." (Pedantic musicologists — there is no other kind — may at this point mention that the proper term for such a madrigal is 'ballet.' Humour them and they may go away.)

Messiah: An oratorio by Handel, attempted every Christmas by some choir that thinks it is good enough, and in collaboration with instrumentalists, who need the money. It is the musical equivalent of death and taxes: inescapable and excruciating.

Mezzo-soprano: A sort of half-hearted Soprano. Marginally more intelligent, due to the reduced effect of high notes, which addle the brain.

Modern Music: The name given in polite company to the present mess we're in. It is important to remember that musical styles are rarely popular when they are new and current, and rarely unpopular when they are old and established. The music of Beethoven, for example, was considered far too 'modern' when it was written. But of course nowadays the music of Beethoven is considered wonderful and great. It is a frightening prospect to consider that the same may be said of today's music, a hundred years from now.

Modes: Groups into which notes were organized before the invention of scales, the introduction of which caused them to become out-moded.

Modulation: A means of getting from one key to another, similar to changing lanes on the highway, and just as hazardous if done recklessly. Unsuccessful modulations may lead to atonality — a sort of twelve-car pile-up.

Music: 1. Any combination of sounds and words, akin to noise and cacophony, produced (intentionally, or by accident) by muscians (also, though rarely, by singers).

2. The printed form of obscure hieroglyphics, squiggles, scrawls, and blots that purport to tell the musician how to produce the desired noise. It may be (a) illegible, (b) boring, (c) too difficult, or (d) any combination thereof. The production of music follows three stages. It is:
1. set down by the composer
2. interpreted (incorrectly) by the conductor, and
3. ignored by the performers and audience.

Music Lesson: A form of cruel and unusual punishment inflicted upon young children by their parents, and upon teachers by their shrinking bank balances. In such instances, it is a debatable point which is more unbalanced — the bank account or the music teacher.

Handel's 'Messiah'

Music Stand: An intricate device for propping up music, except at crucial times — such as during the performance. It has a tendency to fall over, often of its own accord. It comes in two sizes — too high or too low — and it is always broken.

Musica Ficta: Ancient rules for the interpretation of Early Music. A sort of musical *Everyday Etiquette*. In Medieval times, the principles of *ficta* were understood by everybody, so they were never written down. Nowadays, nobody *can* write them down, because nobody understands them at all.

Musicians: Individuals bent upon producing sound or noise by means of scraping, hitting, beating, or blowing into an object made of wood, brass or catgut. In a performance, each may be seen wearing an ill-fitting tuxedo or black dress. (In most cases, the men wear tuxedos and the women wear dresses.) Orchestral musicians are allowed to sit, for which they get paid extra. Choral musicians rarely get paid at all, and they must stand throughout the performance, unless they faint. Most musicians can count to at least four, and some to five. Not to be confused with singers.

The Musician's Union

Musicians Union: A powerful branch of the Mafia that controls the exorbitant amounts of money paid to musicians, and also the number of coffee-breaks permitted per hour (at least one, and usually three, with pay). Singers, not being musicians, are not required to be members. All others must join, the penalty being black-listed, or preferably death.

N

Noise: A more accurate term for sound.

Notes: 1. Little black dots with stems and flags, which are the peculiar language of music. The 'whole' note is divided into 'halves,' 'quarters,' and so on. These divisions are usally referred to as 'long,' 'short,' and 'really short.' Widely held to be understood by musicians (and sometimes by singers), they are, in fact, a bafflement to all — but everyone is too proud to admit it.

Nut: The narrow ridge across the neck of a stringed instrument such as the violin, situated near the pegbox. By extension, then, the term has come to be applied to any person who plays such an instrument.

O

Oboe: An ill wind that nobody blows good.

Octave: A distance of approximately eight notes (twelve if it includes all semi-tones; as many as twenty-seven if sung by a Tenor).

Opera: A performance involving singers with orchestra (complete with unrealistic scenery and silly costumes), which tells a story so complex that nobody in the audience understands what is going on, although all speak about it as if they did. Consists mainly of fat people bellowing in a foreign language.

Opera Buffa: Not, as might be expected, opera performed in the nude. Not yet, anyway.

Orchestra: The result of musicians' having discovered that there is safety in numbers. So much so that the orchestra often out-numbers its audience. Can be distinguished from a mob only by the fact that a mob chooses weapons such as placards and stones, while an orchestra choses weapons such as violins and trumpets. Also, mobs rarely wear black.

Orchestra Pit: 1. A deep hole, in the front of and below the stage, where the orchestra performs, and into which things (including persons) have a tendency to fall.

The Orchestra Pit

2. (Doubtful) That part of an orchestra which is left over when one has digested all of the rest, and which ought to be spat into the garbage (*cf.* cherries, peaches, avocados, *etc.*) or planted. Science has, as yet, been unable to cultivate an orchestra by this method, although some of its failures are no worse than many orchestras already in existence.

Organ: A mythical instrument, part man and part beast, known to inhabit churches — especially ones that are cold, damp, drafty, and impoverished. In constant need of repairs and impossible to tune, it has a very large range: the highest notes attract bats, and the lowest loosen the floorboards. Everything in between sounds like a cross between thunderous cisterns and cold porridge. Most often used to accompany choirs, and to provide background noise for the church service. It can also be an effective means of suppressing sermons.

Organist: The person hired by a church to play the organ and to provide music for services, weddings, funerals, and other joyous occasions. Not to be confused with the organ student, who actually *does* the playing.

Organ student: A species of sub-organist, or a sub-species of organist.

Ornamentation: 1. The practice of adding extra notes to a melody in order to improve it, or to disguise one's inability to perform it properly.

2. The only reason that some persons are allowed to remain in a musical organization.

Ornamentation

P

Passion: 1. One of any number of long-winded oratorios by Bach or others, telling the death and resurrection of Christ. Usually told in the version according to one of the four apostles. *(The Passion According to Reuters' Jerusalem Correspondent* has not received the recognition it deserves.) The performance is ideally suited to the Easter season, since at the end the audience has the feeling of having eaten too many Easter eggs, and the performers feel as if they've laid one.

2. The sort of feeling that is apt to interfere with a musician's practice time, not to mention meals.

Pedal-point: Not to be confused with counterpoint or needlepoint. A compostional device, used especially in pieces for the organ (which badly need it), by which the listener is forwarned that the end is near (of the music, that is). It consists of a long-held note in the bass, sometimes the result of the organist's foot having gone to sleep.

Pedals: A special keyboard on the organ, operated by the player's feet, used for the lowest bass notes. Unlike bicycles and tricycles, which also have pedals, there is little to be gained — and much to be lost — by pedalling the organ as fast as one can.

Pitch

Pencil: This small object is what distinguishes the professional musician from the mere amateur. No self-respecting musician should be without one, and the Union imposes heavy fines on anyone who is unable to produce one, like a Union card, on demand. For this reason, pencils should be zealously guarded, as they have a habit of disappearing. (They often re-appear in the possession of a nearby musician, under circumstances suspiciously resembling theft.) Keeping the pencil *sharp* is another problem altogether — one of the few times that sharpness can be an asset. Courses in this art have recently been introduced at some of the more progressive music schools.

Performance: The main reason for the getting-together of any number of musicians, usually to perform a piece of music (ideally, all at the same time). It is the best excuse for a large, drunken party, although any excuse will do.

Piano: A cumbersome piece of furniture found in many homes, where playing it ensures the early departure of unwanted guests.

Piano Tuner: A person employed to come into the home, re-arrange the furniture, and annoy the cat. The tuner's chief purpose is to ascertain the breaking-point of the piano strings.

Pitch: The relative highness or lowness of a musical note, and the ability to control the same. For an interesting discussion of the curious overlap of terminology between music and baseball, the inquiring reader is referred to the seminal treatise on the subject: *"Das kuriosen Überlappisch Terminologichen zwischen Musik und Baseball und warum es Samstag immer regnet."* *(Munchen: Aschenbecker Verlag)* 1897, rev. 1926.

Podium: A raised platform given to conductors to make them feel more important than they really are. From the podium, the conductor can look over the orchestra and overlook its mistakes.

Polytonality: A pathological disease most likely to affect composers of Modern Music. A mild form of Atonality. Since one of its characteristics is the evidence of a sense of confusion, it is often hard to detect — that being the usual state of many musicians and composers. Nevertheless, this particular confusion tends to manifest itself in a deire to be "all things to all men," at least as regards key and key signature.

Prima Donna: The most important female role in an opera. This is, of course, largely a matter of opinion. By extension, the term has come to be applied to any singer who merely *behaves* as if hers were the important role; that is to say, everyone. Derived from an Italian phrase that may be roughly translated as 'pain in the neck,' although some have a lower opinion.

A Prodigy

Prodigy: A person who shows tremendous musical talent at a very early age. Mozart, one of music's greatest proigies, set the example that was to be followed by others, by dying at age thirty-six. Those wishing to be considered prodigy material would be well advised to die young, before it becomes apparent that they aren't going to get any better, and while the reduced Union rates for children still apply.

Programme Notes: Short essays, filled with useless and unverified (*i.e.* untrue) information about composers and their music, provided as a supplement to a performance. They are intended to furnish insight into the music, on the fanciful theory that a well-informed audience is an appreciative audience. In fact, it is probably better to keep audiences in the dark — figuratively speaking. They are already literally in the dark, which makes it impossible to read the programme notes anyway. At any rate, all of this is a moot point, since the programme will be changed at the last minute, and it will bear no relation to what is written in the notes.

Q

Quartet: All that remains of the Moscow Philharmonic Orchestra after its North American tour.

Quaver: What many performers do while performing.

R

Recitative: Gossip set to music. A device in opera and oratorio for getting large chunks of narration over with quickly. Unfortunately, this leaves more time to be spent on long-winded arias.

Reeds: A family of instruments that includes the clarinet, oboe, bassoon, and kazoo. The name derives from the material that vibrates to produce the sound. Many reeds would be better off left in a swamp.

Refrain: 1. The part of a song which keeps being repeated, *ad nauseam*.

   2. What most performers should do.

Rehearsal: Ideally, a meeting of musicians (and singers) for the purpose of becoming familiar with the music. In fact, a social occasion where little if any work is done. Most useful for the repetition of mistakes.

Rehearsal Letter: A letter of the alphabet written into the score and the individual parts of a piece of music. The placement of the letter corresponds to the number of the bar, and is intended as a reference-point, to facilitate rehearsal. That's the theory, anyway. Unfortunately, the letter often appears at a different place in each part, leading to mass confusion.

Repertoire: The large number of standard pieces of music with which an orchestral musician must claim to be familiar in order to secure a position in a major orchestra. Also, the pieces that a singer is

A Rest

likely to forget at any given time. The American Civil War hero General Ulysses S. Grant made the definitive comment on repertoire when he remarked: "I only know two tunes. One of them is *Yankee Doodle*. The other one isn't."

Rest: 1. A short period of relative silence in an individual part, useful for turning pages, breathing, cleaning out spit-valves, coughing, and so forth. Rarely found in Baroque music, Union regulations now exist to govern the number of rests required in each piece of music (usually one per bar, or fifteen minutes of every hour).

Rhythm: 1. A faculty in great demand and, unfortunately, in very short supply among those involved in music.

2. An unreliable method for curtailing the population of musicians.

Rubato: The term used to describe the erratic behaviour of a performer in the throes of anguish brought on by the mating season. Especially prevalent in Tenors.

Runs: An ailment particularly prevalent among singers of Baroque music, especially that of Bach and Handel. Can often be remedied by proper diet.

S

Score: An amalgamation of all of the individual parts, transposed into the key of C, so that no one else can understand it. This is what conductors conduct from, and they are supposed to have studied it carefully. Most conductors, however, don't know the score.

Serial Music: Not to be confused with early morning, or cereal, music. The result of a method of composition using all twelve notes of the scale in some established order. Despite this, the result is often chaos.

Sharp: 1. Adjective used to describe a tone that is slightly above-pitch (*cf.* Flat: not so easily misconstrued).

2. Adjective used to descibe a nattily-attired colleague.

Sharps: Little marks that look like this: # and which would be useful for playing Xs and Os during the more boring moments of a performance if they were not so small. They are similar to flats, but different. Their function is to raise a note by a semi-tone (more or less). They also may be gathered to form key signatures. For an explanation of the double-sharp, read the entry for Flats and figure it out for yourself. There may be a short quiz at the end of this book.

Singer: A special type of musician, notable for the inability to count at all. Unlike other musicians, who must rely upon the instrument to produce sound, singers use only the vocal apparatus (what ordinary people would call 'the voice'). There are certain inherent advantages and disadvantages: on the one hand, a singer wishing to improve his or her technique cannot simply buy a better instrument — but then some of the carrying-cases are so much more attractive. Singers are usually paid less than instrumentalists (if at all), and usually remain standing throughout the performance. Often, someone will faint.

Snob, Musical: A person who pretends to know more about music than we pretend to.

Solo: A device that makes it easier to place the blame for mistakes entirely upon one individual. The other device that facilitates this is called the Conductor.

Soloists: Individuals whose egos are larger than both their brains and ability combined, and equalled in some cases only by their greed. Soloists can be of two types, either (a) good, or (b) bad. The latter are more common. In fact, the former exist only in theoretical treatises, and have never been known to exist in real life. Certainly never in real performances.

Sonata Form:　　The development of Sonata Form (also called Sonata Allegro Form or First Movement Form) is one of the most fascinating topics in the study of music, since it combines elements of history, theory, analysis, and composition. It also involves all of the major composers of Western music. We wish we had more time to talk about it.

Soprano:　　The highest vocal line, sung by women (but *cf.* Treble). Sopranos have a tendency to sing sharp, and to sound like finger-nails scraped on chalkboard. Derived from the Latin *superius*, which means 'highest.' This has given many Sopranos a superiority complex, exceedingly unfounded. Sopranos tend to be the most feeble-minded of all the singing voices. This may be explained by the fact that notes of higher frequency travel directly to the brain (but see Brain) and cause rapid decay.

Sound:　　1. A polite term for noise.

　　　　2. A type of mental attitude rarely obtained by musicians, even more rarely by conductors, and never by singers.

Stop:　　1. A device on the organ, which changes the sound of a note from disagreeable to annoying.

　　　　2. What organists should do to improve their playing (*cf.* refrain).

Stringendo: Also string-endo: the term applied to a demised violin.

Strings: 1. A family of instruments that includes the violin, viola, cello, double-bass, and yo-yo. The strings used in producing the sound were originally manufactured out of catgut. This may be responsible for their ear-piercing tone, which continues even in these days of synthetic string material. Ancient violin makers believed that the best strings were made from female cats in heat, as evidenced by the violin's characteristic screech.

A Soaprano

T

Temperament: 1. A set of guidelines for tuning instruments, chiefly keyboards.

2. The state of mind that quickly deteriorates when such guidelines are applied incompetently.

Tempo: The speed at which music travels. Said to be controlled by the conductor, but in reality by the players. It may vary from piece to piece, and certainly from player to player. It is always faster in performance than it has been in rehearsal, usually by a factor of two.

Tenor: A high-pitched male voice, akin to screaming. Extremely rare, so usually sung by frustrated Baritones whose reach exceeds their grasp. Tenors have a tendency to sing off-pitch, out of time, out of control, and to sound like a strangulating cat. Derived from the Latin *tenor*, which means 'to hold' (*cf.* tenacious, tenuous, tentative).

Tone: 1. That aspect of a singer's performance which may be complimented when one could not understand the words (*cf.* diction).

2. The interval of the distance between two adjacent notes. Can be either of a whole tone or a semi-tone. Occasional use of quarter-tones has not been successful, since musicians have difficulty dealing with fractions smaller than halves.

Tone-cluster: A kind of chordal orgy, a smorgasbord of musical tones. First discovered by a very well-endowed lady pianist, while leaning forward to turn a page.

Tonic: A medicinal libation usefully consumed before a performance; even more usefully so afterwards.

Transposition: 1. The act of moving the relative pitch of a piece of music that is too low for the Basses up to a point where it is too high for the Sopranos.

2. A method of ensuring that no musician will be able to read a part belonging to another musician, by writing each part in a different key. Through some miracle not as yet understood by theorists, the parts usually sound right together. The conductor retaliates by transposing everything into the key of C (see Score) to confuse the musicians, and because that is the only key that most conductors can read, even a little bit. The main purpose of transposition is to provide work for copyists.

Treble: A small boy used especially in Anglican Church choirs to sing the highest vocal line (under other circumstances sung by a Soprano). Those who favour this type of choral sound mantain that all the effort it takes to properly train small boys is worthwhile, because the end result is so pleasing, and because they are usually the boys' mothers. In addition to the usual skills of sight-reading and interpretation that must be learned, boys must be taught forms of self-discipline such as bladder control. Often, the former is easier than the latter.

Triangle: 1. A small instrument used by percussionists chiefly to annoy the rest of the orchestra.
2. A romantic configuration not advised for musicians wishing to avoid heartache, embarrassment, financial ruin or legal proceedings.

Trill: The musical equivalent of an epileptic seizure.

Trio Sonata: An instrumental piece popular in the Baroque, so called because it has parts for four players. This is the same sort of logic that accounts for the theorist's calling the combined intervals of an octave and a third a tenth. ($8 + 3 = 10$ — what could be more sensible than that?). The inherent fallibility of this reasoning has not seemed to dismay musicians over the centuries, so we should not let it trouble us now. Strangely enough, musicians' inability to count properly disappears whenever they are calculating their wages.

Trombone: A slide-whistle with delusions of grandeur.

Tuxedo: A type of ill-fitting black suit worn by male musicians during a performance. It is purchased at a local Salvation Army store (or — preferably — borrowed from another musician) and must be at least ten years old. It is either too large or too small, too baggy or too tight. Footwear accompanying the tuxedo is very occasionally a pair of black dress shoes (rarely polished), but more often sneakers, brown loafers, or sandals. The addition of a questionably white shirt and a bowtie (either black, or rainbow-coloured) completes the outfit. The ownership of a tuxedo is mandatory for musicians — much like a fez for Shriners. The female equivalent of the tuxedo is any dress, knee-length or longer, which is vaguely black (i.e. black, grey, brown, blue, purple, chartreuse, *etc.*).

Vibrato

V

Valve: A means of changing the direction of the flow of air in the tube of a brass instrument. Similar to a highway detour, but less likely to require a map.

Variation: The sort of tune written by composers who can never make up their minds.

Verismo: A style of writing opera that attempts to make the characters and situations more life-like and realistic. Since the terms 'opera' and 'realism' are mutually exclusive, verismo — like Santa Claus and the Tooth Fairy — can never really exist at all.

Vibraphone: A xylophone with stage-fright.

Vibrato: A technique used by certain instruments, said to add warmth and body to the tone, and used by singers to hide the fact that are on the wrong pitch.

Viol: One of a family of bowed stringed instruments, popular in the Renaissance, that became the forerunners of the modern violin family. Opinion is divided on which of the two instruments, ancient or modern, is more vile than the other.

Viola: A relative of the violin, a sort of poor cousin.

Violin: The squeakiest member of the string family. It tends to get its way in an orchestra because violins outnumber the other instruments.

Virginal: A keyboard instrument similar to the harpsichord, so called because of the sorts of ladies who were supposed to play it in the 16th century — and if you believe that, you'll believe anything.

Voluntary: The name given to a piece for organ often played at the end of a church service. The terminology is puzzling and ironic, since under such circumstances one's decision to endure the assault is far from voluntary.

W

Wind: The essential ingredient needed to produce sound from many instruments. It is possessed in large quantities by conductors, who have very little need for it.

Woodwinds: A family of instruments so called because its members are made of wood. This includes the flute (which is made of silver), the saxophone (made of brass), and the bassoon (which is often made of plastic). The woodwind family includes all the members of the reed family, as well as others, such as the flute, that would otherwise feel left out. Like most families, the members often quarrel.

Wrong Notes: It must be understood that this is a relative term, and applies only to those examples performed by someone else. Wrong notes performed by oneself are always referred to as 'ornaments'.

Woodwind

X

Xylophone: An instrument of the percussion family. Its chief claim to fame is that its name begins with an 'x' — the only instrument so honoured. Consequently, it is extremely useful for compilers of musical dictionaries.

Z

Z: The sound made by members of the audience during a performance (especially of opera). Usually found in the plural, thus: ZZZZZZ. Often accompanied by a snore.

Other books by David W. Barber and Dave Donald

BACH, BEETHOVEN, AND THE BOYS
Music History As It Ought To Be Taught
(1986)

WHEN THE FAT LADY SINGS
Opera History As It Ought To Be Taught
(1990)

IF IT AIN'T BAROQUE
More Music History As It Ought To Be Taught
(1992)

by Dave Donald

HECTOR AND THE BIG HOUSE
(1977)

A Musician's Dictionary

First published in Canada by

Sound And Vision
359 Riverdale Avenue
Toronto Canada M4J 1A4

First printing August 1983
23.21.19.17.15 printings 14.16.18.20.22
99.97.95.93 year 94.96.98

Canadaian Cataloguing in Publication Data
Barber, David W. (David William), 1958 -
A musician's dictionary.

ISBN 0-920151-03-5

1. Music - Terminology - Anecdotes, facetiae,
satire, etc

Printed and bound in Canada on acid free paper